Why things don't work
RACING CAR

www.raintreepublishers.co.uk
Visit our website to find out more information about
Raintree books.

To order:
☎ Phone 44 (0) 1865 888112
📄 Send a fax to 44 (0) 1865 314091
💻 Visit the Raintree bookshop at
www.raintreepublishers.co.uk to browse our
catalogue and order online.

Why things don't work RACING CAR
was produced by

David West 👥 **Children's Books**
7 Princeton Court
55 Felsham Road
London SW15 1AZ

Editor: Dominique Crowley
Consultant: Michael Bayley

First published in Great Britain by
Raintree, Halley Court, Jordan Hill, Oxford OX2 8EJ, part of
Harcourt Education. Raintree is a registered trademark of Harcourt
Education Ltd.

10 digit ISBN: 1 4062 0547 8
13 digit ISBN: 978 1 4062 0547 3

11 10 09 08 07
10 9 8 7 6 5 4 3 2 1

British Library Cataloguing in Publication Data

West, David
    Racing car. - (Why things don't work)
    1.Automobiles, Racing - Maintenance and repair - Comic
    books, strips, etc. - Juvenile literature
    I.Title
    629.2'8728

Printed and bound in China

Why things don't work
RACING CAR

by David West

Contents

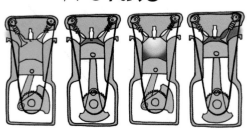

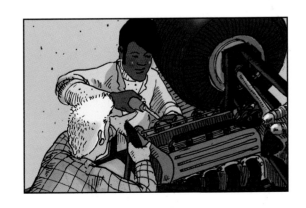

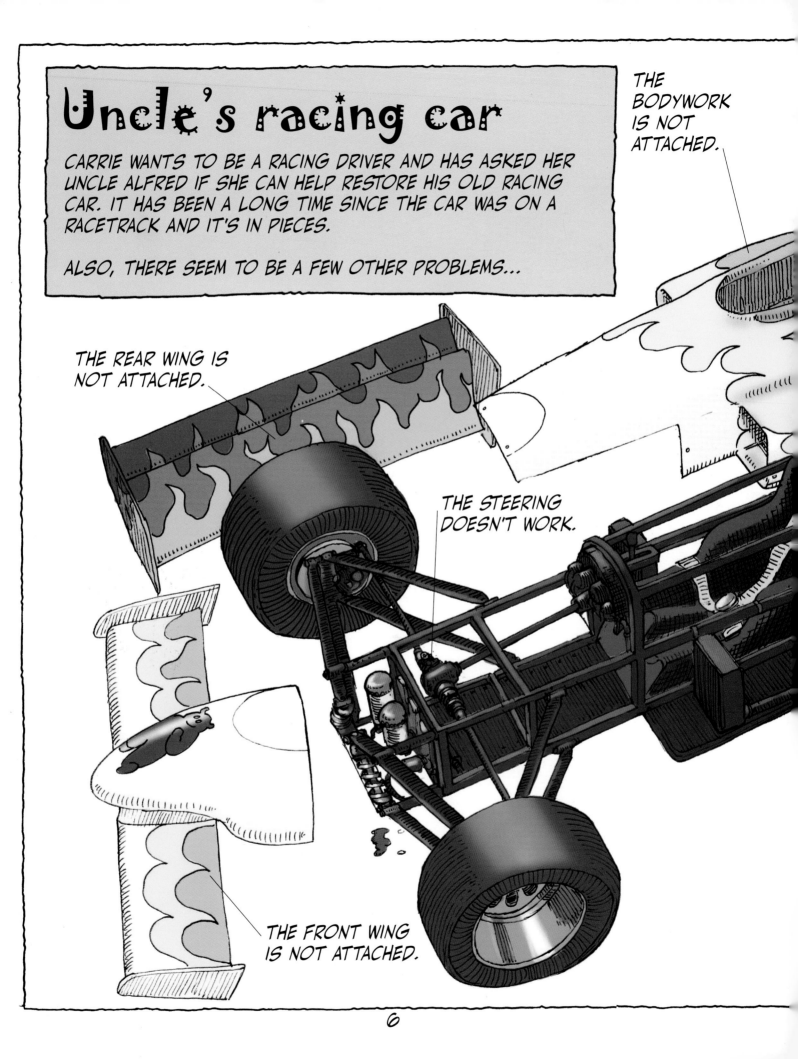

Uncle's racing car

CARRIE WANTS TO BE A RACING DRIVER AND HAS ASKED HER UNCLE ALFRED IF SHE CAN HELP RESTORE HIS OLD RACING CAR. IT HAS BEEN A LONG TIME SINCE THE CAR WAS ON A RACETRACK AND IT'S IN PIECES.

ALSO, THERE SEEM TO BE A FEW OTHER PROBLEMS...

THE BODYWORK IS NOT ATTACHED.

THE REAR WING IS NOT ATTACHED.

THE STEERING DOESN'T WORK.

THE FRONT WING IS NOT ATTACHED.

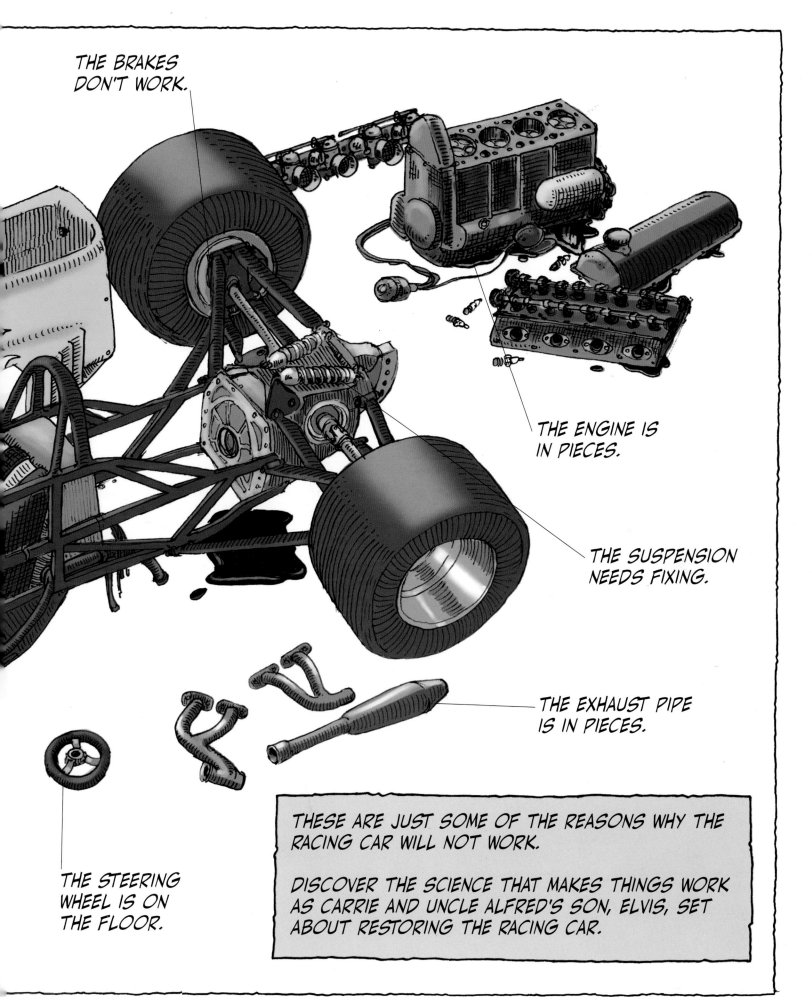

THE BRAKES
DON'T WORK.

THE ENGINE IS
IN PIECES.

THE SUSPENSION
NEEDS FIXING.

THE EXHAUST PIPE
IS IN PIECES.

THE STEERING
WHEEL IS ON
THE FLOOR.

THESE ARE JUST SOME OF THE REASONS WHY THE
RACING CAR WILL NOT WORK.

DISCOVER THE SCIENCE THAT MAKES THINGS WORK
AS CARRIE AND UNCLE ALFRED'S SON, ELVIS, SET
ABOUT RESTORING THE RACING CAR.

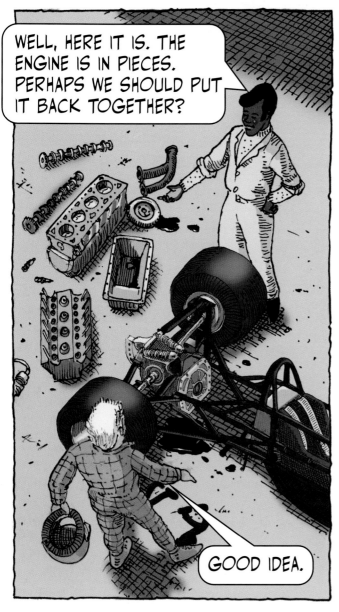

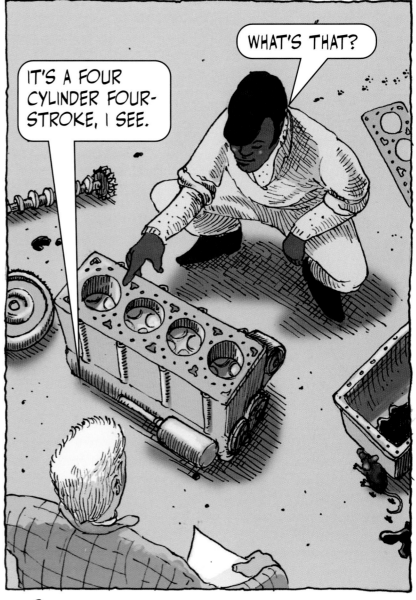

LOOK, I'LL SHOW YOU.

Cam Head Spark plug
Valve Cam
Valve
Inlet port Exhaust
port
Cylinder Piston
Cam chain
Crankshaft

THESE ARE THE MAIN PARTS OF THE ENGINE.

THERE ARE THE FOUR CYLINDERS AND YOU CAN SEE THE **PISTON** HEADS.

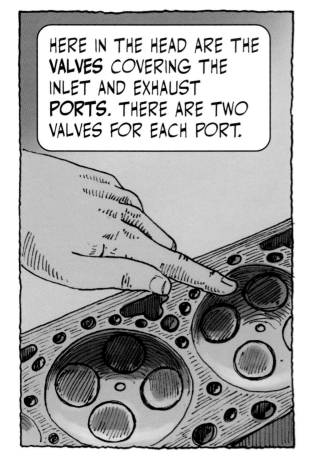

HERE IN THE HEAD ARE THE **VALVES** COVERING THE INLET AND EXHAUST **PORTS**. THERE ARE TWO VALVES FOR EACH PORT.

AND HERE ARE THE **CAMS** ON ONE OF THE TWO CAMSHAFTS.

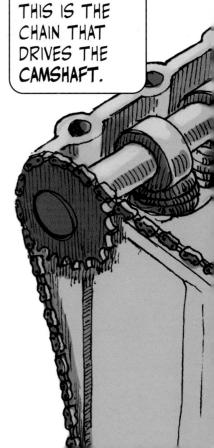

AND SEE HERE? THIS IS THE CHAIN THAT DRIVES THE **CAMSHAFT**.

9

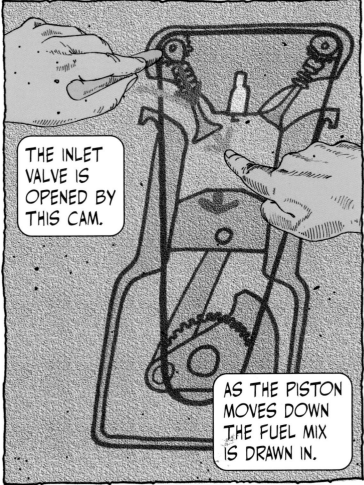

10

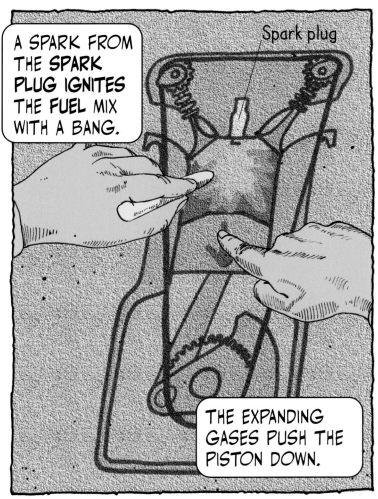

A SPARK FROM THE **SPARK PLUG** IGNITES THE **FUEL MIX** WITH A BANG.

Spark plug

THE EXPANDING GASES PUSH THE PISTON DOWN.

THE PISTON MOVES UP AGAIN AND THE **EXHAUST GASES** ARE FORCED OUT.

THIS CAM ROTATES TO OPEN THE EXHAUST VALVE.

THEN WHAT?

IT ALL STARTS AGAIN. THE PISTON GOES DOWN, UP, DOWN, UP, FOR EVERY BANG. THAT'S FOUR STROKES PER BANG.

SO THAT'S WHY IT'S CALLED A FOUR-STROKE.

YES.

WHAT ARE THOSE LITTLE HOLES FOR?

SOME CARRY THE OIL AND SOME CARRY THE WATER AROUND THE ENGINE.

OIL MAKES THE SURFACES OF THE MOVING PARTS SLIPPERY, HELPING TO CUT DOWN **FRICTION**. IT ALSO HELPS TO COOL THEM.

YIKES! I SEE WHAT YOU MEAN. THIS OIL IS VERY SLIPPERY.

THE WATER RUNS THROUGH TUBES IN THE ENGINE'S CASING AND ALSO CARRIES AWAY HEAT. THE WATER IS COOLED BY AIR RUSHING THROUGH RADIATORS IN THE SIDE PODS.

HOW DOES THE WATER GET TO THE RADIATORS?

Radiator

Water pump

Engine

IT IS PUSHED THROUGH PIPES BY THE WATER PUMP. COOLED WATER RETURNS TO THE ENGINE FROM THE RADIATORS.

WE HAD BETTER START PUTTING IT TOGETHER.

I THINK WE ARE GOING TO NEED YOUR DAD'S HELP.

UNCLE ALFRED HELPED US REBUILD THE ENGINE AND ATTACH IT TO THE FRAME OF THE RACING CAR.

WHAT'S THIS UNIT RIGHT AT THE BACK?

CLANK

THAT'S THE **GEAR BOX**. IT TRANSFERS POWER FROM THE ENGINE TO THE REAR WHEELS.

INSIDE THE GEAR BOX IS A SET OF GEARS, LIKE THESE.

AS YOU CAN SEE, THEY FIT TOGETHER NEATLY.

OH, YES.

HOW DO YOU CHANGE GEARS?

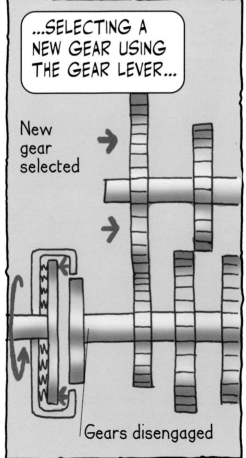

YOU SEPARATE THE POWER FROM THE ENGINE TO THE GEARS WITH THE **CLUTCH**. BY PRESSING DOWN THE CLUTCH PEDAL...

Power from the engine

Clutch

Crankshaft | Gears disengaged

...SELECTING A NEW GEAR USING THE GEAR LEVER...

New gear selected

Gears disengaged

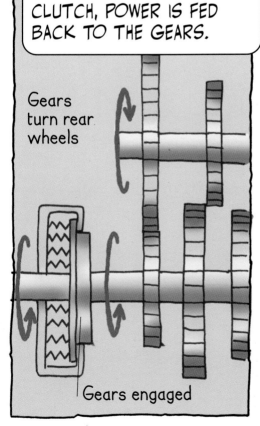

...AND RELEASING THE CLUTCH, POWER IS FED BACK TO THE GEARS.

Gears turn rear wheels

Gears engaged

THE DIFFERENT ARRANGEMENTS OF THE GEARS MAKE THE WHEELS TURN FASTER OR SLOWER. JUST LIKE ON A BICYCLE.

THE GEAR BOX HAS ANOTHER INTERESTING PART TO IT. THERE IS A DEVICE CALLED THE DIFFERENTIAL.

AS A CAR GOES AROUND A CORNER, THE OUTSIDE WHEEL TRAVELS FURTHER THAN THE INSIDE WHEEL.

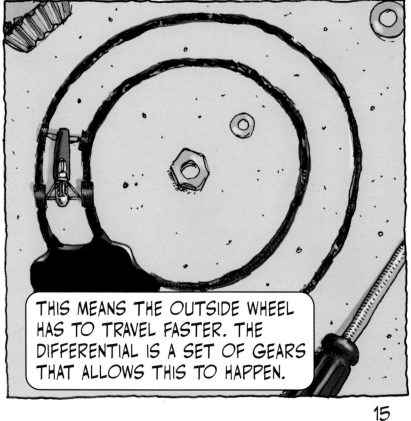

THIS MEANS THE OUTSIDE WHEEL HAS TO TRAVEL FASTER. THE DIFFERENTIAL IS A SET OF GEARS THAT ALLOWS THIS TO HAPPEN.

I'LL LEAVE YOU TO PUT THE REST OF IT TOGETHER.

THAT'S THE EXHAUSTS FITTED. NOW WE NEED TO ATTACH THE CARBURETTORS.

WHAT DO THE CARBURETTORS DO?

YOU'LL NEED TO ATTACH THE FUEL LINE AND THE THROTTLE **CABLE** TO THE CARBURETTORS.

FUEL WON'T BURN WITHOUT AIR. CARBURETTORS MIX THE FUEL AND AIR TOGETHER.

Air/fuel mix to engine

Fuel in

Air in

WHEN YOU PRESS THE **THROTTLE** PEDAL, THE VALVE LETS IN MORE OF THE MIXTURE TO THE ENGINE. THIS MAKES THE EXPLOSIONS STRONGER, SO THE ENGINE GOES FASTER.

More air/fuel mix to engine

Air in

Throttle valve fully open

Fuel in

16

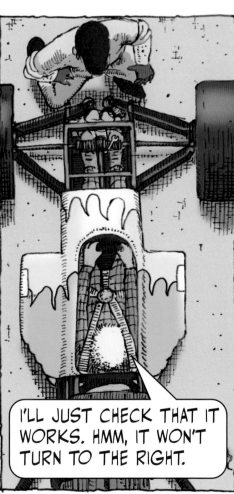

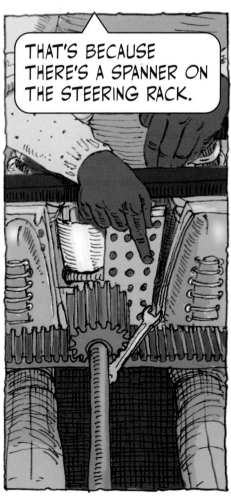

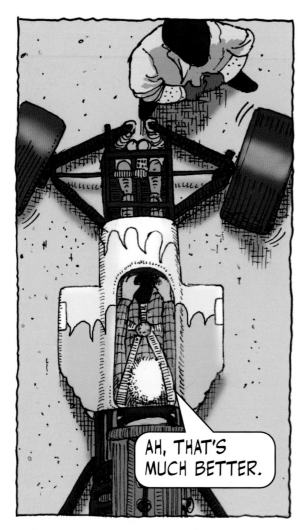

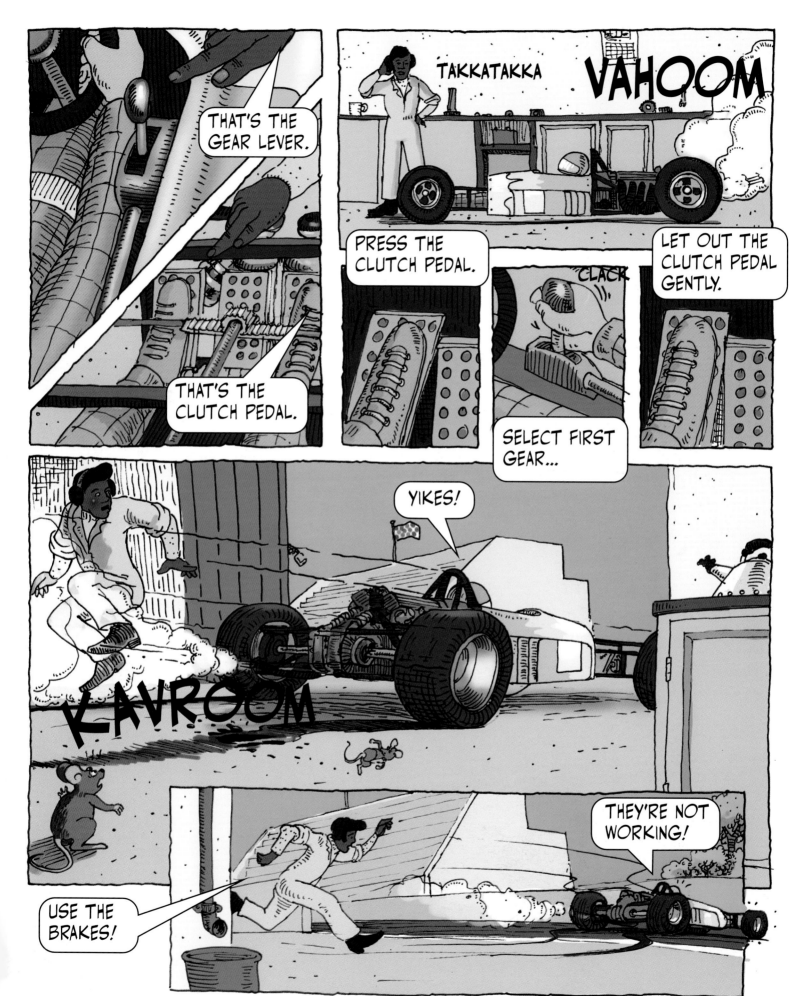

19

CRASH

YIKES!

ARE YOU OK?

YES. THE TYRES AND HAY SOFTENED THE BLOW.

LET'S WHEEL IT BACK TO THE PITS.

BACK AT THE PITS...

WHEN YOU PRESS THE BRAKE PEDAL, IT PUSHES A PISTON IN A CYLINDER FILLED WITH BRAKE FLUID.

Brake fluid reservoir

Brake pedal

Brake cylinder

Brake piston

Brake fluid to brakes

THE FLUID PUSHES PISTONS WITH PADS AGAINST METAL DISCS ATTACHED TO THE WHEELS.

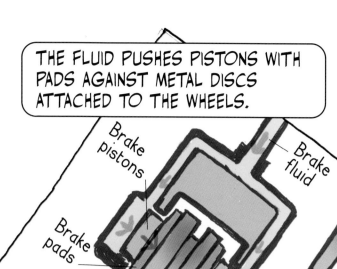

Brake pistons

Brake fluid

Brake pads

Brake disc

Wheel

THE PADS PRESS AGAINST THE DISCS, WHICH CREATES FRICTION. THIS SLOWS DOWN THE WHEELS.

WE CHECKED ALL THE PADS IN THE BRAKES.

WELL, WE'VE REPLACED ALL THE PADS BUT THE BRAKES STILL DON'T WORK.

PERHAPS THERE'S NO BRAKE FLUID IN THE PIPES?

YOU'RE RIGHT. THE BRAKE FLUID RESERVOIR IS EMPTY.

LOOK, THE PIPE HERE IS LOOSE.

WE TIGHTENED THE PIPE AND FILLED UP THE RESERVOIR WITH BRAKE FLUID.

THAT'S BETTER. THE BRAKES WORK NOW.

21

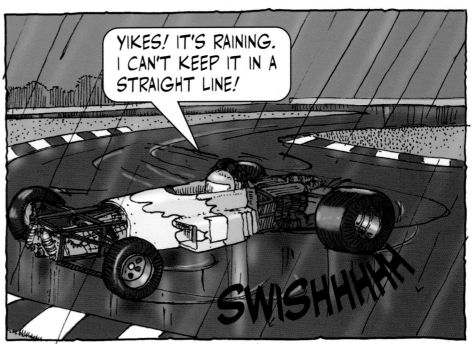

22

LOOK HERE. THE SPRING AND DAMPER CAN BE SET TO DIFFERENT LEVELS.

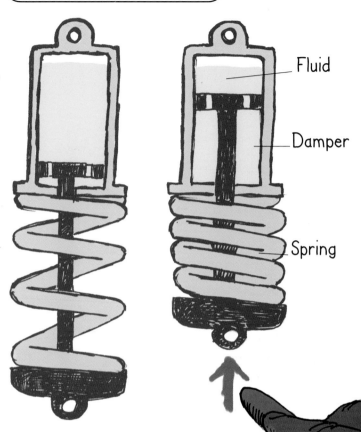

THE SPRING CUSHIONS THE SHOCK OF A BUMP.

Fluid

Damper

Spring

THE DAMPER HAS FLUID IN IT, WHICH SLOWS DOWN THE MOVEMENT OF THE SPRING. THIS STOPS THE SPRING BOUNCING TOO MUCH.

THAT SHOULD DO IT. TAKE THE CAR OUT AGAIN AND SEE IF IT HANDLES BETTER.

WE CHANGED THE SETTINGS ON THE SUSPENSION SO THAT THE CAR WAS LESS BOUNCY. EACH WHEEL HAD ITS OWN SUSPENSION.

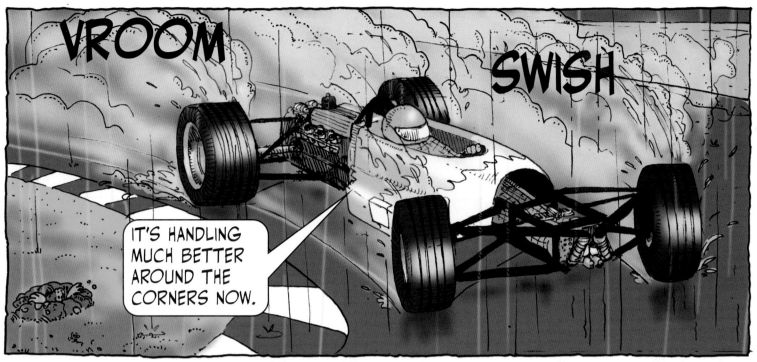

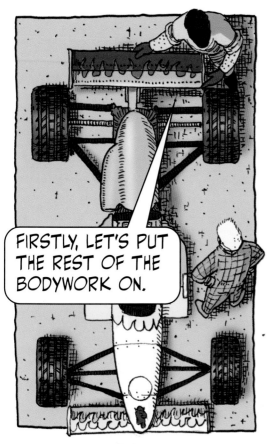

FIRSTLY, LET'S PUT THE REST OF THE BODYWORK ON.

AS YOU CAN SEE, THERE ARE WINGS FITTED ON BOTH THE FRONT AND REAR OF THE CAR.

WOW! DOES THAT MEAN IT CAN FLY?

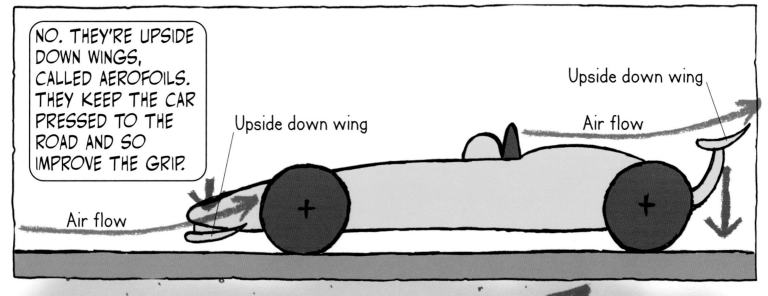

NO. THEY'RE UPSIDE DOWN WINGS, CALLED AEROFOILS. THEY KEEP THE CAR PRESSED TO THE ROAD AND SO IMPROVE THE GRIP.

Upside down wing

Upside down wing

Air flow

Air flow

AIR RUSHING UNDER THE AEROFOIL HAS FURTHER TO TRAVEL THAN THE AIR ON THE TOP. THIS CAUSES IT TO FLOW MORE QUICKLY THAN THE AIR ON THE TOP.

Slow air flow

Aerofoil

Fast air flow

Low pressure area

THIS CREATES A LOW PRESSURE AREA UNDER THE AEROFOIL, WHICH PULLS THE AEROFOIL DOWNWARDS.

LOOK, I CAN SHOW YOU HOW IT WORKS WITH THIS PIECE OF PAPER.

THE PAPER REPRESENTS THE AEROFOIL. WHEN I BLOW OVER IT...

...THE AEROFOIL MOVES UP.

THIS IS WHAT HAPPENS ON THE CAR WINGS. EXCEPT THEY ARE UPSIDE DOWN.

THE CAR WORKED REALLY WELL. THE AEROFOILS HELPED IT TO GRIP THE ROAD. THE BODYWORK SEEMED TO MAKE THE CAR SLIP THROUGH THE AIR MORE EASILY.

ZOOOOM

UNCLE ALFRED SAID THERE WERE LOTS OF DIFFERENT TYPES OF RACING CARS. SO WE WENT TO SEE SOME.

WE WENT TO SEE A FORMULA ONE CAR BEING BUILT.

WOW! THESE FORMULA ONE CARS LOOK REALLY SLEEK.

THEY USE THE LATEST TECHNOLOGY IN THESE CARS. A WIND TUNNEL SHOWS HOW THE AIR FLOWS OVER THE CAR.

WE WENT TO SEE A RALLY CAR EVENT.

I BET THEY NEED REALLY STRONG SUSPENSION.

WE SAW A NASCAR RACE.

WHY DO THEY GO INTO THE PITS?

THEY NEED TO CHANGE THEIR OUTSIDE WHEELS, WHICH GET WORN OUT ON THIS OVAL TRACK.

28

WE WENT TO SEE DRAGSTERS RACING OVER A STRAIGHT QUARTER MILE.

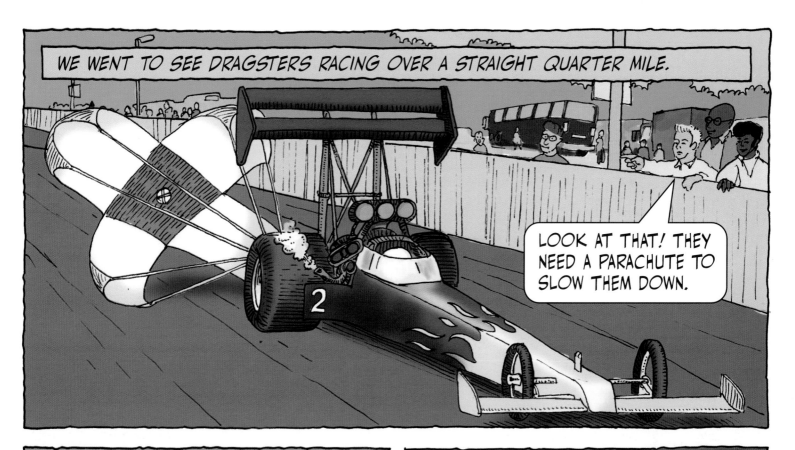

LOOK AT THAT! THEY NEED A PARACHUTE TO SLOW THEM DOWN.

AT ANOTHER EVENT WE WATCHED, THE CARS WERE ALLOWED TO BASH INTO EACH OTHER.

I CAN SEE WHY THEY CALL IT A DEMOLITION DERBY.

THE BEST EVENT, THOUGH, WAS THE ONE I ENTERED, KART RACING.

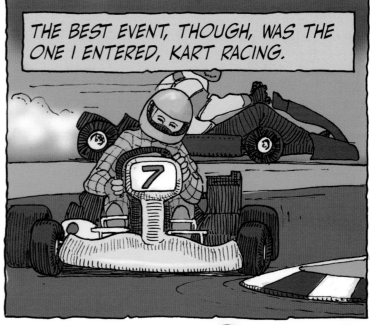

WELL DONE! THAT'S YOUR FIRST WIN. YOU'RE ON YOUR WAY TO BEING A RACING CAR DRIVER.

Parts of a racing car

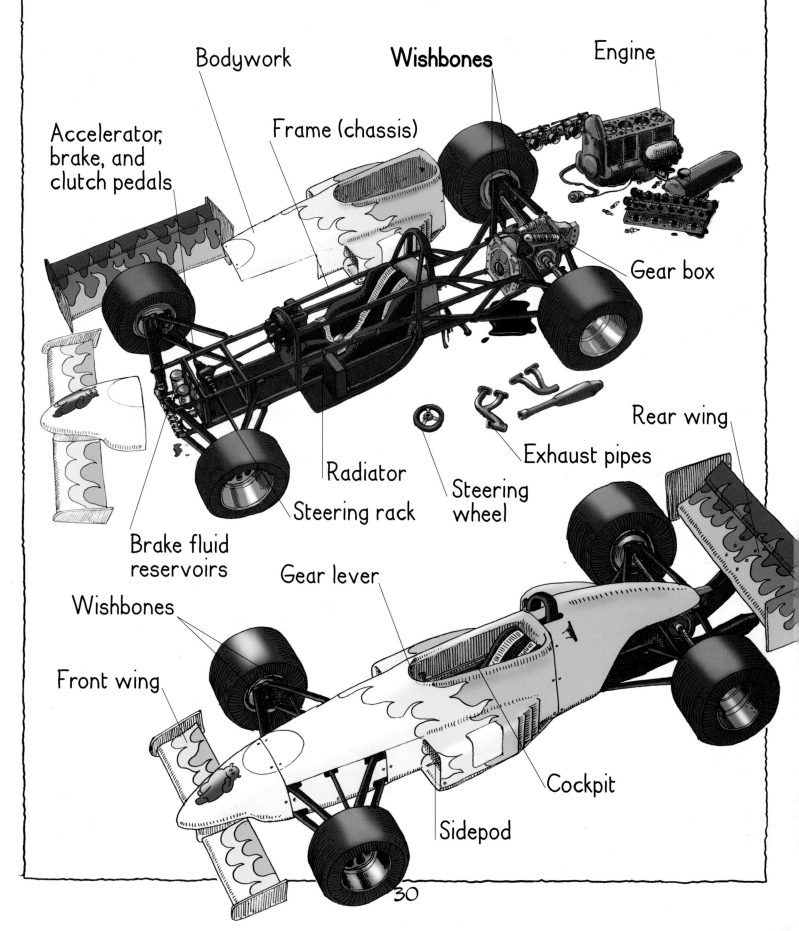

Bodywork

Wishbones

Engine

Accelerator, brake, and clutch pedals

Frame (chassis)

Gear box

Radiator

Steering rack

Steering wheel

Exhaust pipes

Rear wing

Brake fluid reservoirs

Gear lever

Wishbones

Front wing

Cockpit

Sidepod

Glossary

CABLE
A FLEXIBLE WIRE TO OPERATE THE CARBURETTOR

CAM
OVAL-SHAPED METAL PIECES THAT ROTATE. THEY HIT THE TOP OF A VALVE AND PUSH IT DOWN, WHICH OPENS UP A PORT.

CAMSHAFT
ROTATING ROD OR SHAFT ON WHICH THE CAMS ARE FIXED

CLUTCH
A DEVICE THAT DISCONNECTS THE GEARS FROM THE ENGINE SO THAT YOU CAN CHANGE A GEAR

CRANKSHAFT
THE ROTATING SHAFT IN THE BOTTOM OF AN ENGINE THAT IS TURNED BY PISTONS

EXHAUST GASES
FUMES THAT ARE CREATED BY THE EXPLODING FUEL/AIR MIXTURE IN THE ENGINE

FRICTION
THE RESISTANCE CAUSED BY TWO SURFACES RUBBING AGAINST EACH OTHER. IT ALWAYS CREATES HEAT.

FUEL
MATERIAL THAT IS BURNED TO GIVE POWER. RACING CAR FUEL IS MADE FROM OIL.

GEAR BOX
THE CASE FOR THE GEARS

GLASS FIBRE
A MATERIAL MADE FROM STRANDS OF GLASS AND GLUE, WHICH CAN BE FORMED INTO A RIGID, STRONG BUT LIGHT SHAPE

IGNITE
TO SET ALIGHT

PISTON
A METAL CYLINDER WITH ONE CLOSED END THAT MOVES TO AND FRO INSIDE ANOTHER CYLINDER

PITS
THE AREA AT THE SIDE OF A RACETRACK WHERE RACING CARS CAN BE REPAIRED

PORT
AN OPENING, USUALLY WITH A VALVE IN IT

SPARK PLUG
A DEVICE IN THE TOP OF AN ENGINE'S CYLINDER THAT CREATES A SPARK TO IGNITE THE FUEL/AIR MIXTURE

THROTTLE
THE DEVICE TO CONTROL THE AMOUNT OF FUEL INTO THE ENGINE, AND HENCE HOW FAST OR SLOWLY IT WILL RUN

VALVE
A DEVICE THAT OPENS TO ALLOW A LIQUID OR GAS THROUGH IN ONE DIRECTION

WISHBONES
THE TUBES THAT CONNECT THE WHEELS TO THE BODYWORK, SO CALLED BECAUSE THEY LOOK LIKE A CHICKEN'S WISHBONE

Index